Activity Book

My Little Island

1

Leone Dyson

Pearson Education Limited
Edinburgh Gate
Harlow
Essex CM20 2JE
England
and Associated Companies throughout the world.

www.pearsonelt.com

© Pearson Education Limited 2012

The moral rights of the author have been asserted.

All rights reserved; no part of this publication may be reproduced, stored in a retrieval system, or transmitted in any form or by any means, electronic, mechanical, photocopying, recording, or otherwise without the prior written permission of the Publishers.

First published 2012
Eleventh impression 2019

ISBN: 978-1-4479-1357-3

Set in Fiendstar

Printed in Slovakia by Neografia

Illustrated by José Luis Briseño

Contents

1. Welcome 4
2. My Class 10
3. My Family 16
4. My Room 22
5. My Toys 28
6. My Face 34
7. Food 40
8. Animals 46
9. My Garden 52

Practice with Sounds 58

1 Welcome

1 Colour and say.

Practice: *hello, hi, Kimmy*

Practice: *hello, hi, Timmy*

STORY PRACTICE

2 Trace and colour. Say.

Practice: *I'm (Timmy)* .

3. **Colour and say.**

Practice: draw, listen, sing

UNIT 1

④ **Trace and colour. Say.**

Practice: dance

5 Trace and colour. Say.

Practice: stand up, sit down

2 My Class

1 Match, colour, and say.

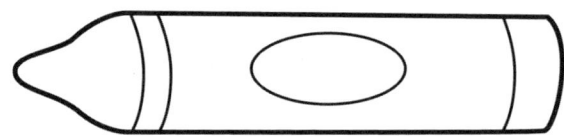
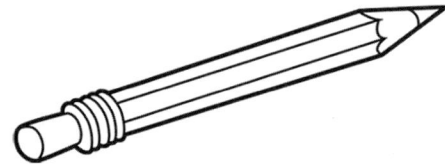
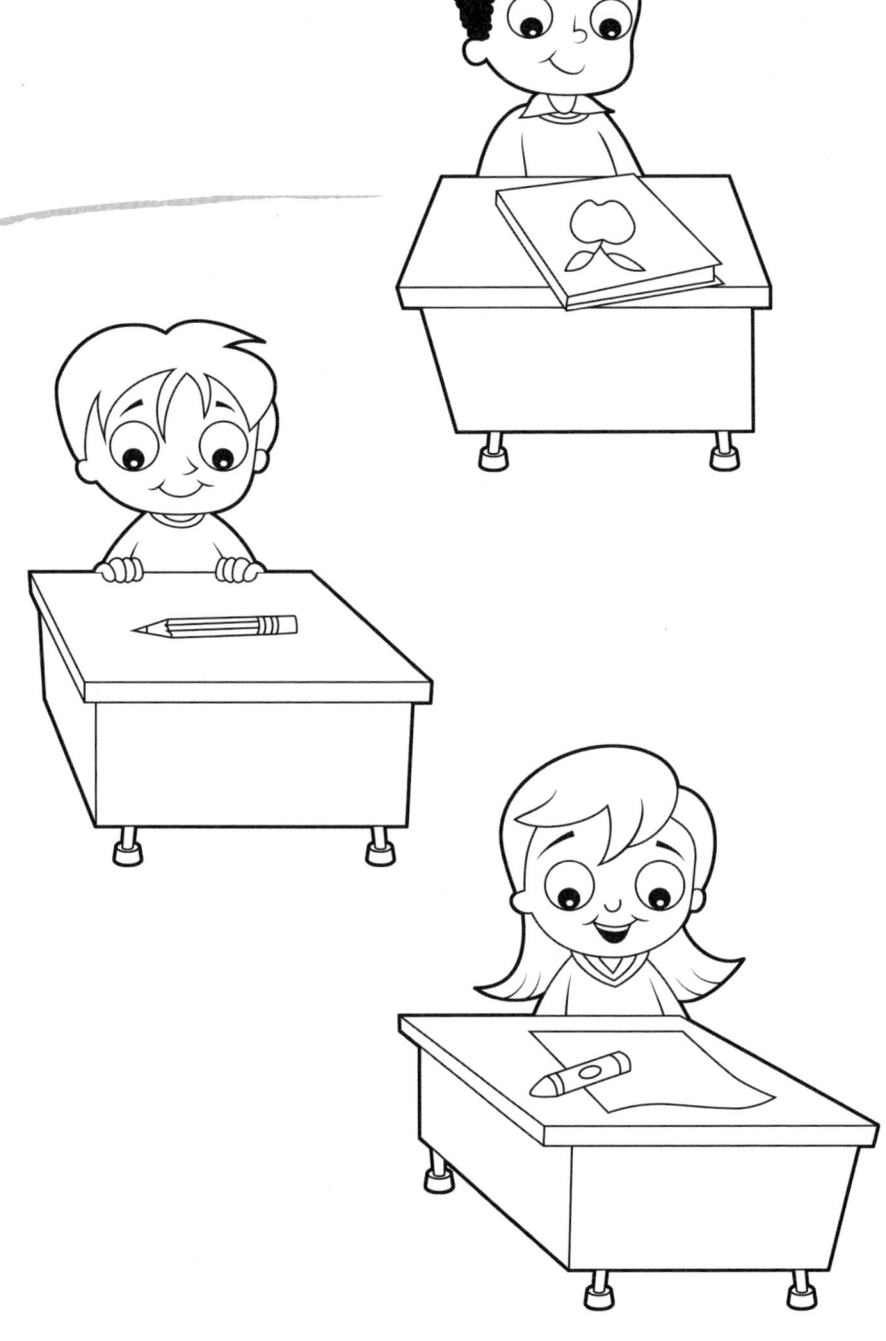

Practice: *book, crayon, pencil*

STORY PRACTICE

2 Follow the paths. Colour and say.

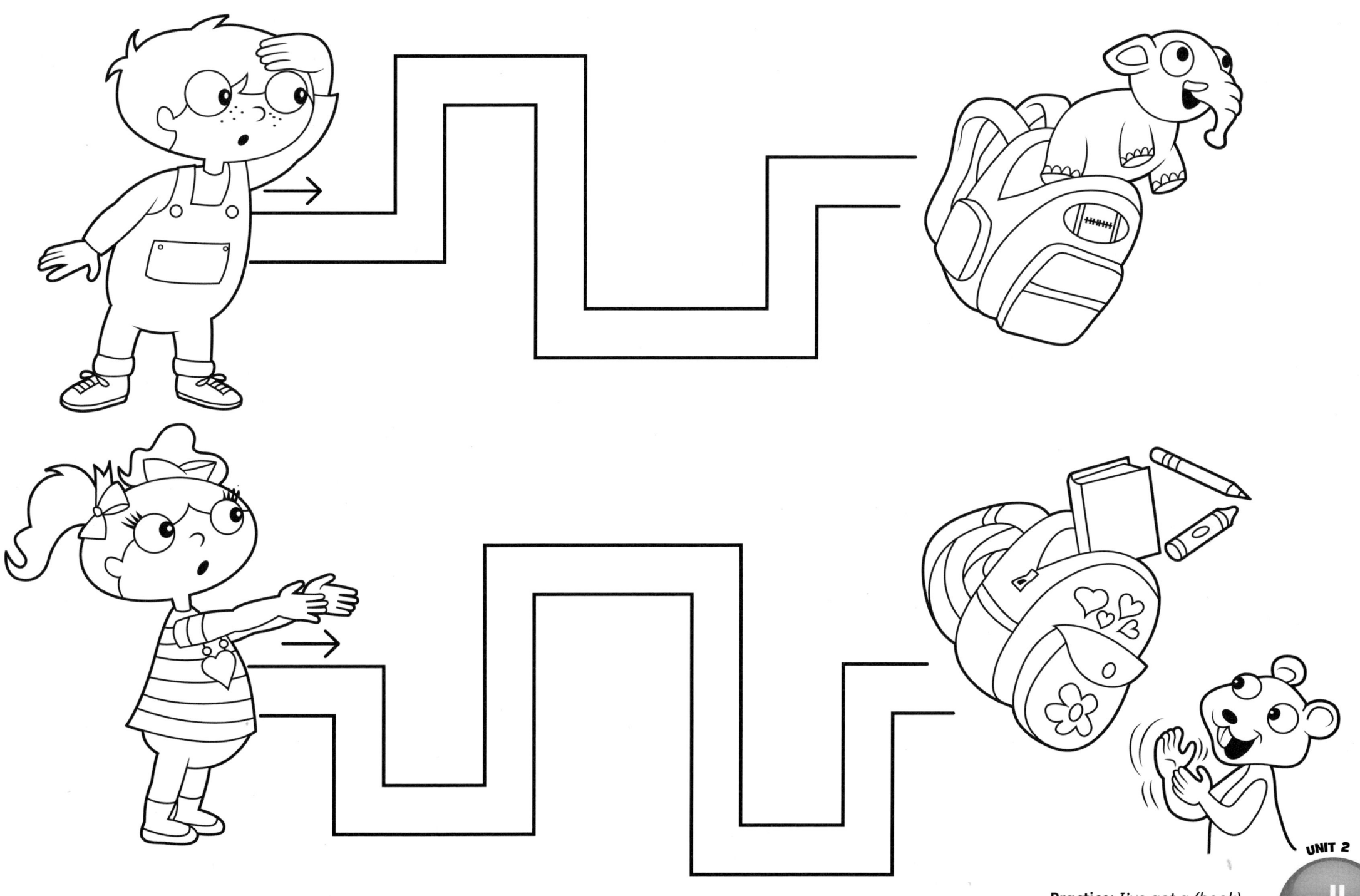

Practice: *I've got a (book).*

3 **Colour red.**

Practice: *book, red*

4 Trace and colour.

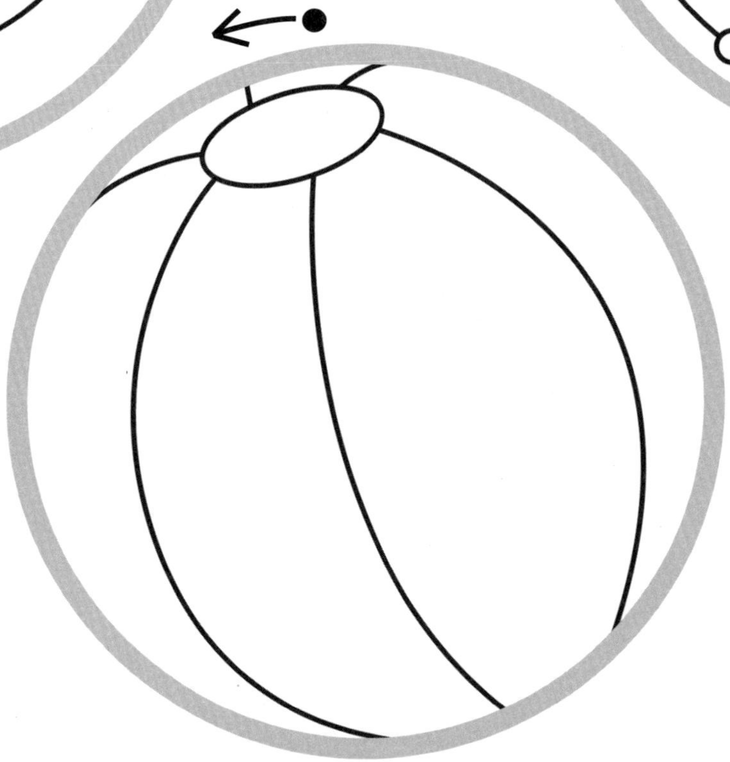

Practice: *circle*

UNIT 2

13

VALUES

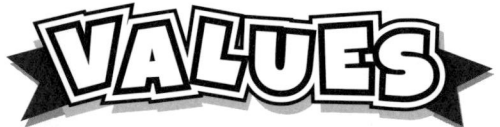

5 **Colour the books and say.**

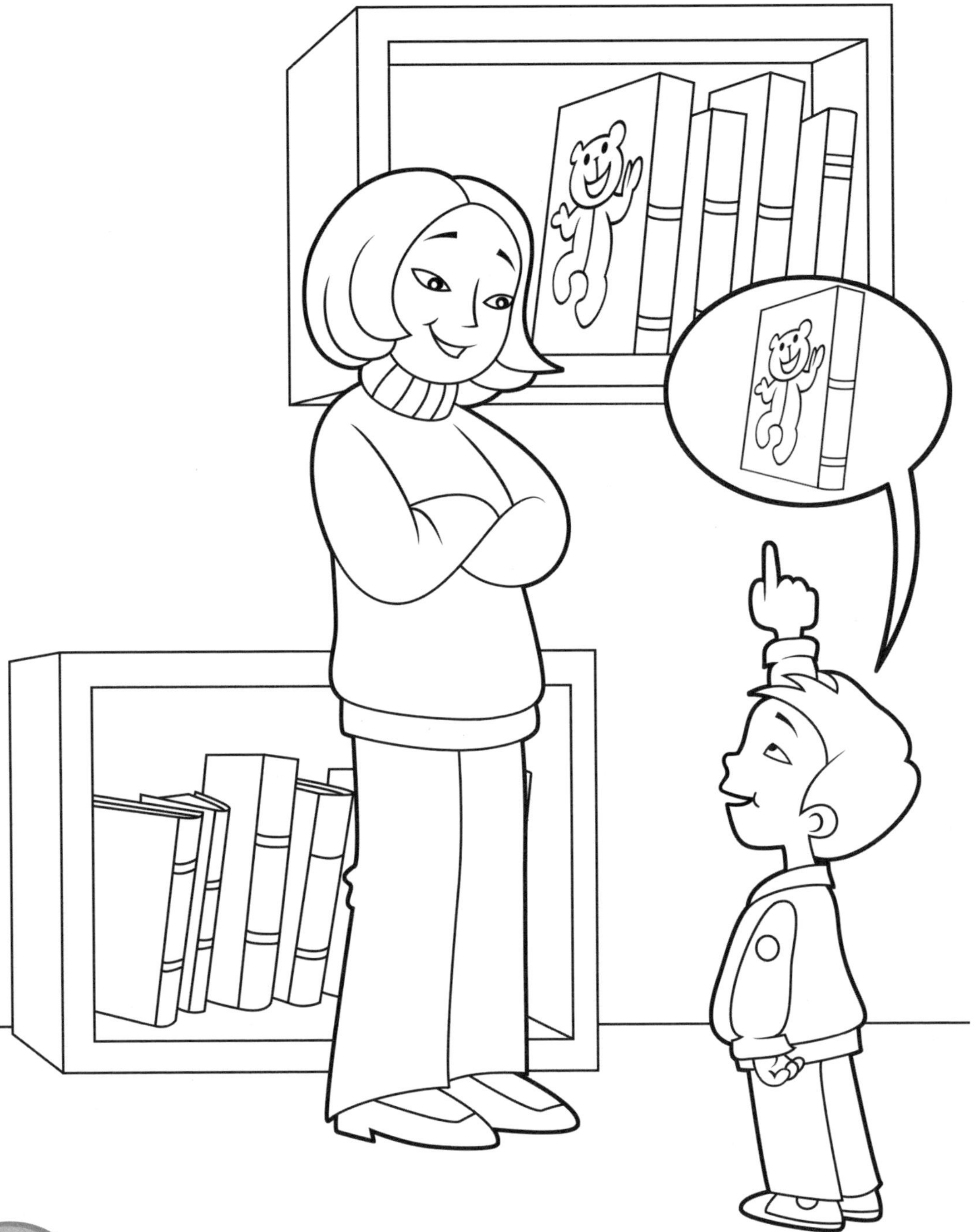

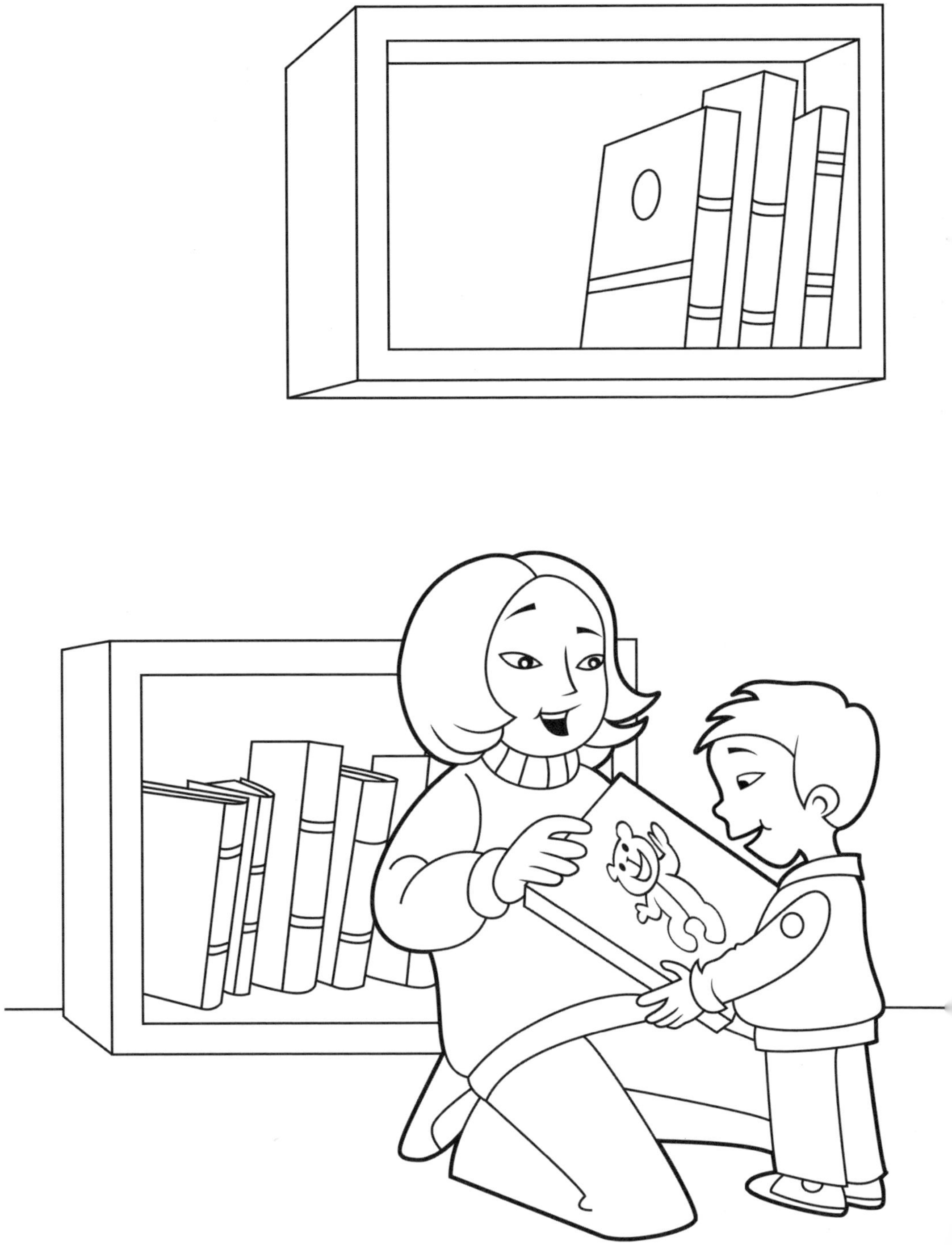

Practice: Ask nicely.

REVIEW

6 **Draw and colour. Say.**

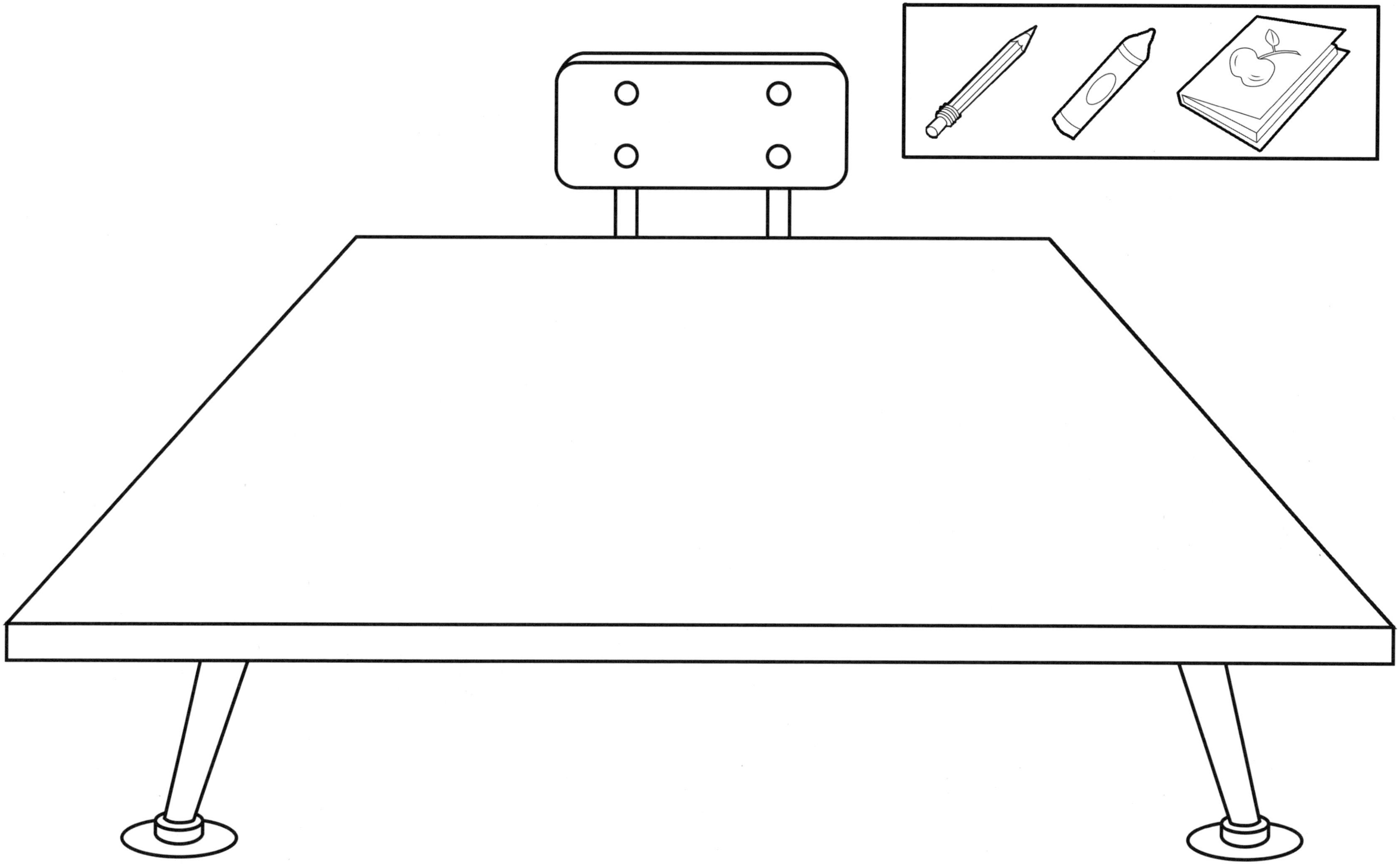

Review: *I've got a (book).*

3 My Family

1 Match, colour, and say.

Practice: *dad, mum, family*

STORY PRACTICE

2 Follow the paths. Colour and say.

Practice: *This is my (sister).*

UNIT 3

3 **Colour blue and red.**

Practice: *baby, blue* Review: *red*

④ **Trace and colour.**

Practice: *brother, dad, mum, sister, triangle*

UNIT 3

19

VALUES

5) **Colour and say.**

Practice: Say *sorry*.

REVIEW

6 Draw your family. Colour and say.

Review: *This is my (family).*

4 My Room

1 Match, colour, and say.

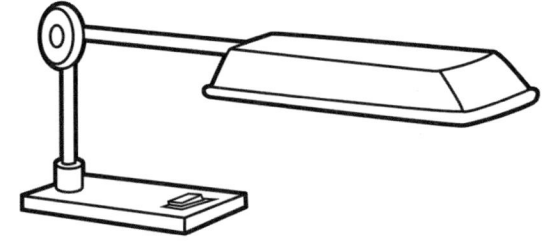
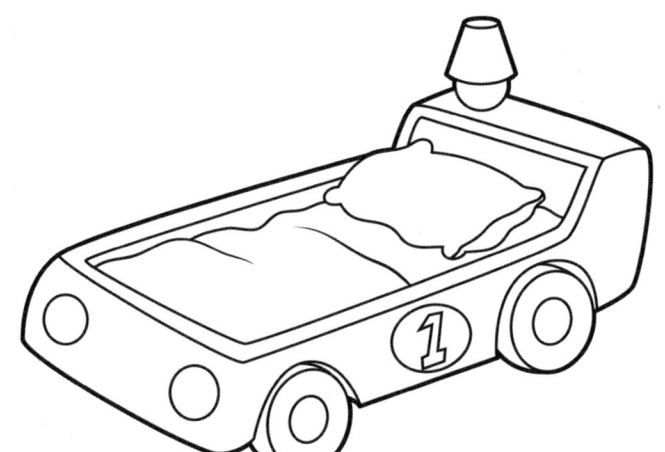

Practice: *bed, clock, lamp*

STORY PRACTICE

2 Trace, colour, and say.

Practice: *It's a (house).*

3 Colour green.

Practice: *green, toy box*

④ **Trace and colour.**

Practice: *bed, clock, door, lamp, square, toy box, window*

UNIT 4

VALUES

5) **Trace, colour, and say.**

Practice: Help others.

Draw and colour. Say.

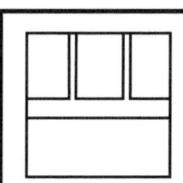
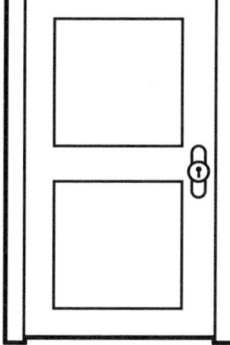
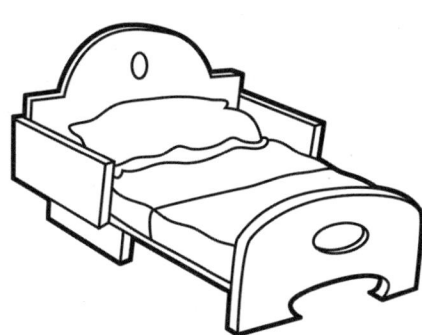

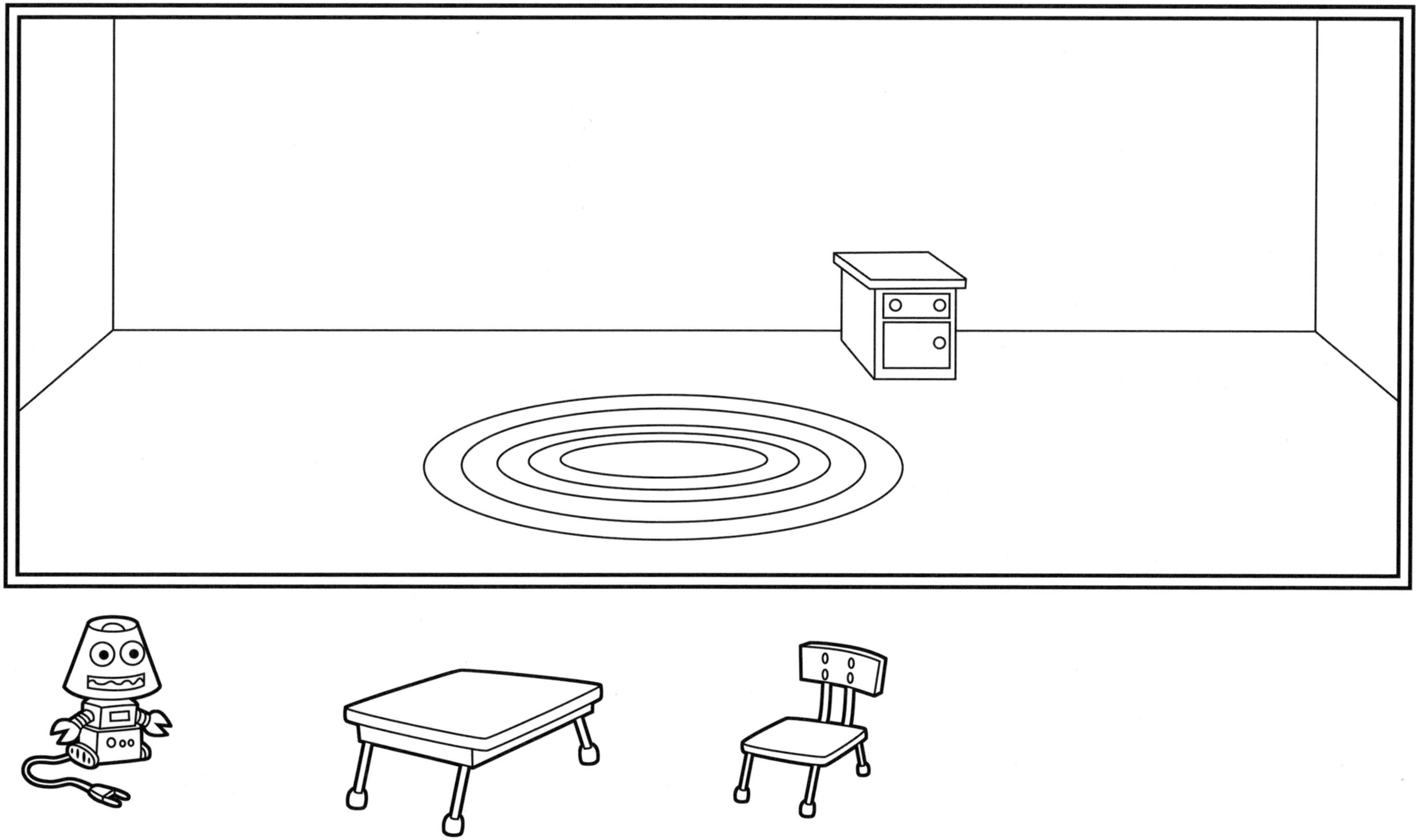

Review: *It's a (lamp).*

UNIT 4

5 My Toys

1 Find and colour. Say.

Practice: *ball, blocks, doll, kite*

STORY PRACTICE

2 Match, color, and say.

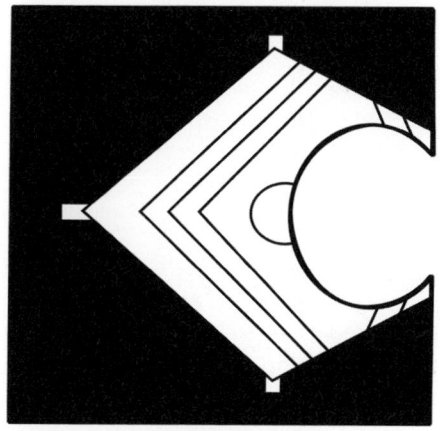
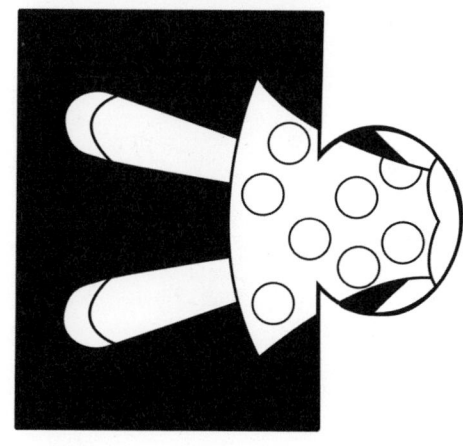

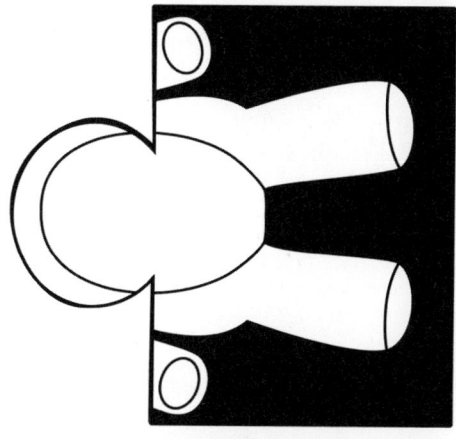
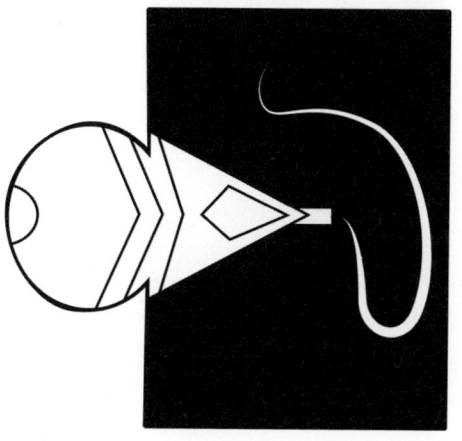

Practice: *I've got a (kite). It's (yellow).*

UNIT 5

3 Colour yellow.

Practice: *puzzle, yellow*

4 **Match, colour and say.**

1

2

3

Practice: 1–3, doll, kite, teddy bear

VALUES

5 Trace, colour, and say.

Practice: Put away your toys.

REVIEW

6 Draw and colour. Say.

UNIT 5

Review: *I've got a (ball). It's (yellow).*

# 6 My Face

1 Trace and colour. Say.

Practice: *ears, eyes, face, hair, mouth, nose*

3 **Colour brown.**

Practice: *brown*

4) **Match, colour and say.**

1
2
3
4

VALUES

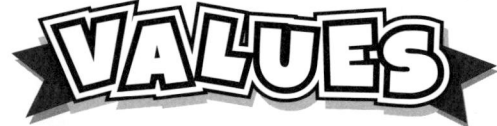

5 **Join 1–4. Colour and say.**

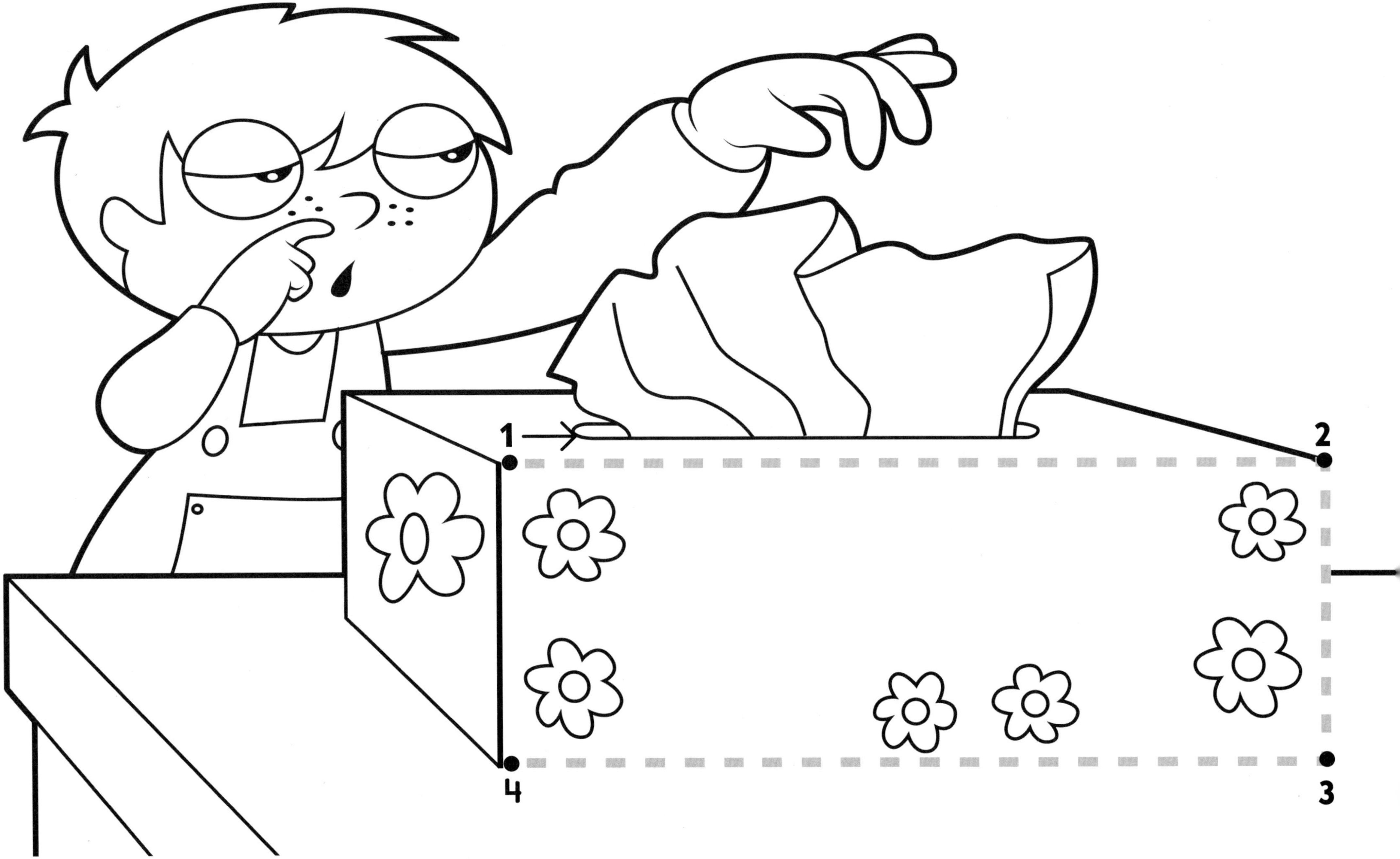

Practice: Cover your nose and mouth.

7 Food

1 Match, colour, and say.

Practice: *cake, cheese, juice*

3 Colour orange.

Practice: *orange*

4 Count and match. Colour and say.

3

4

5

UNIT 7

Practice: *3–5, cheese, milk, yoghurt*

43

Draw a ☺ or ☹. Colour and say.

Review: *I like/don't like (cheese).*

UNIT 7

8 Animals

1 Trace and colour. Say.

Practice: *bird, cat, dog, fish, mouse, turtle*

STORY PRACTICE

2 Colour and say.

UNIT 8

Practice: *The dog is (blue).*

47

3 Colour purple.

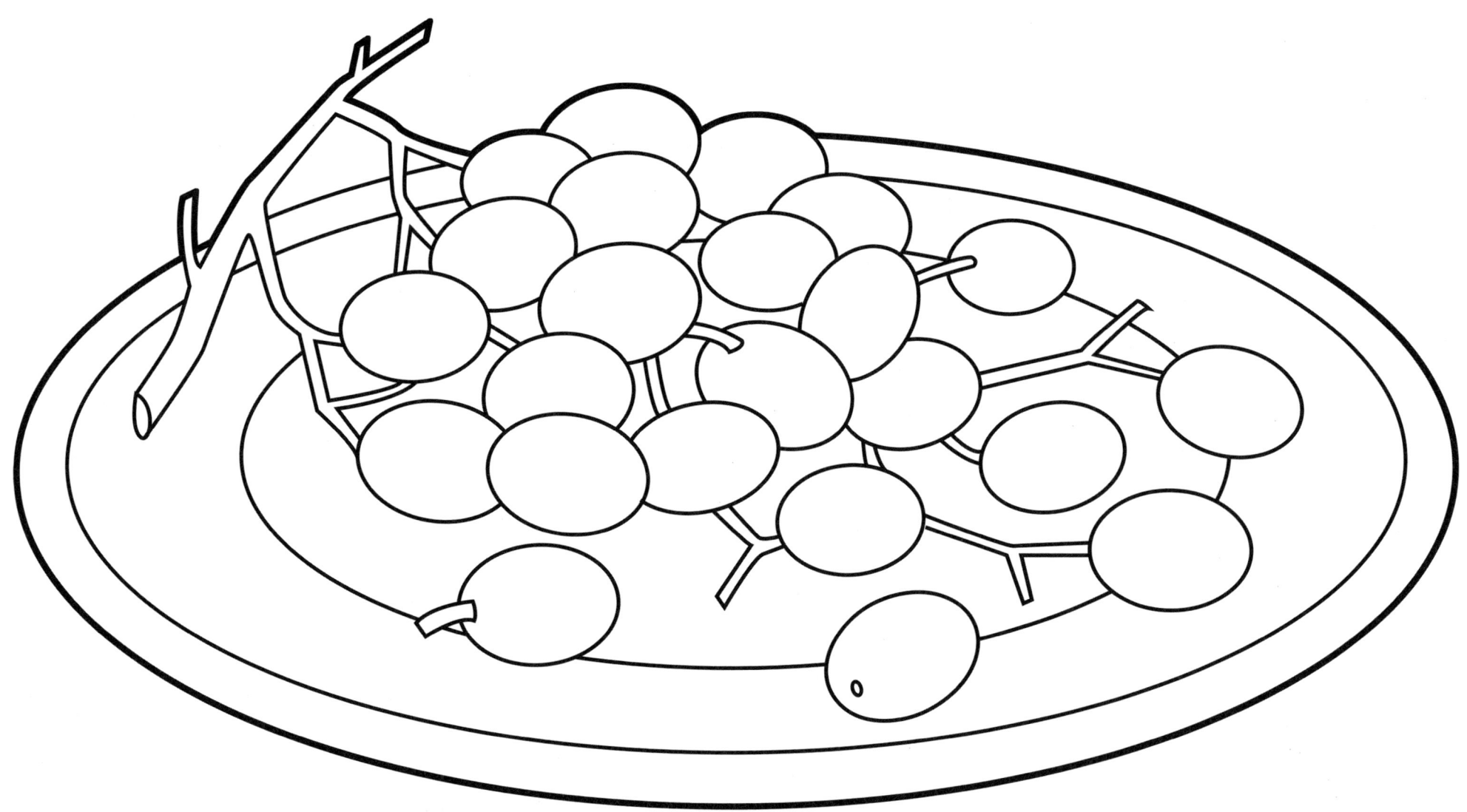

4 **Count and match. Colour.**

1   2   3   4   5

Practice: *1–5, bird, cat, dog, mouse, turtle*

VALUES

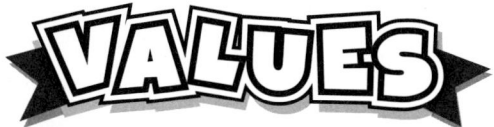

5 **Trace, colour, and say.**

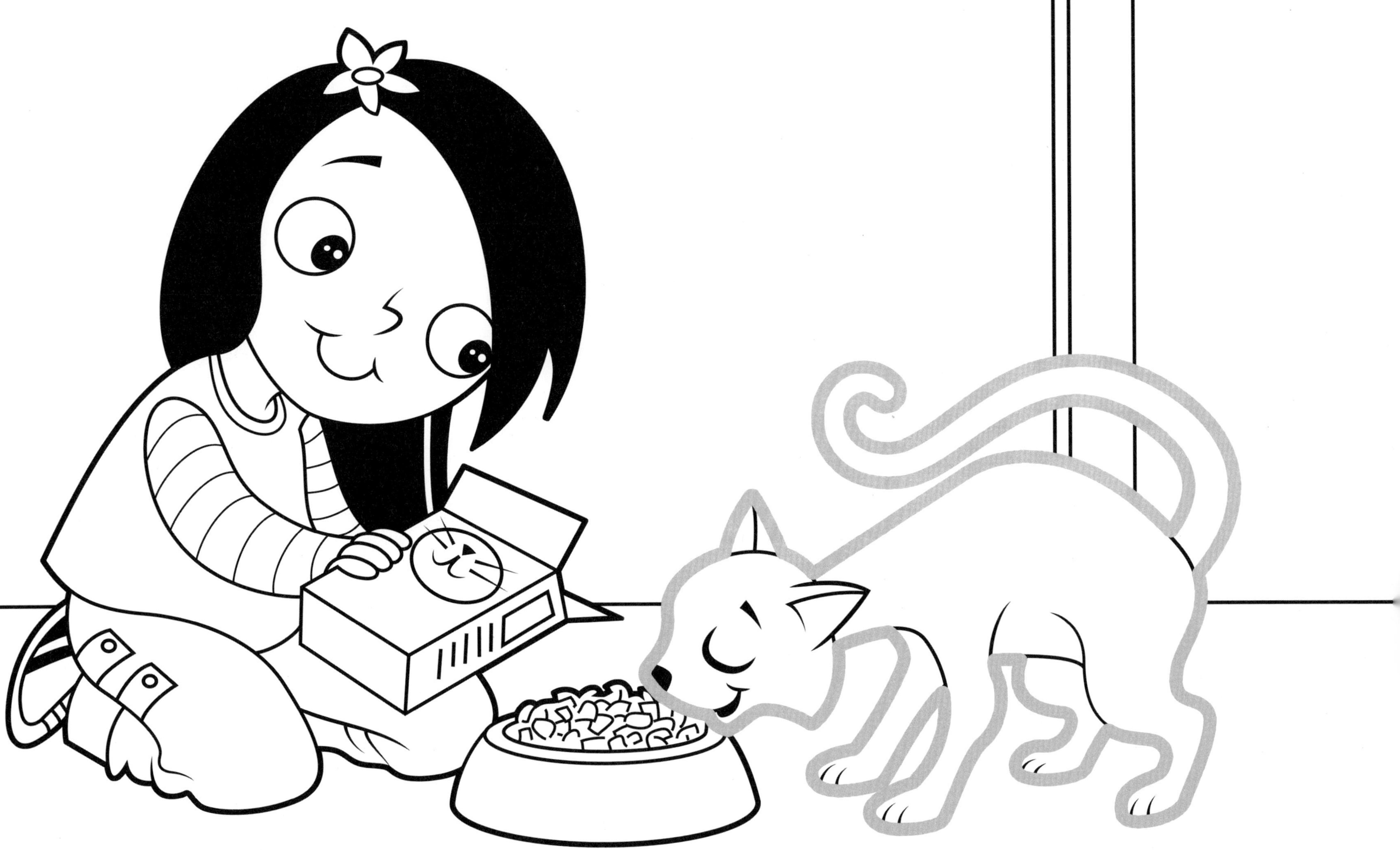

Practice: Be nice to animals.

REVIEW

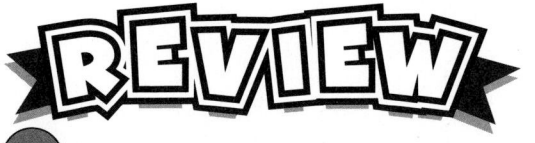

6 Draw and colour. Say.

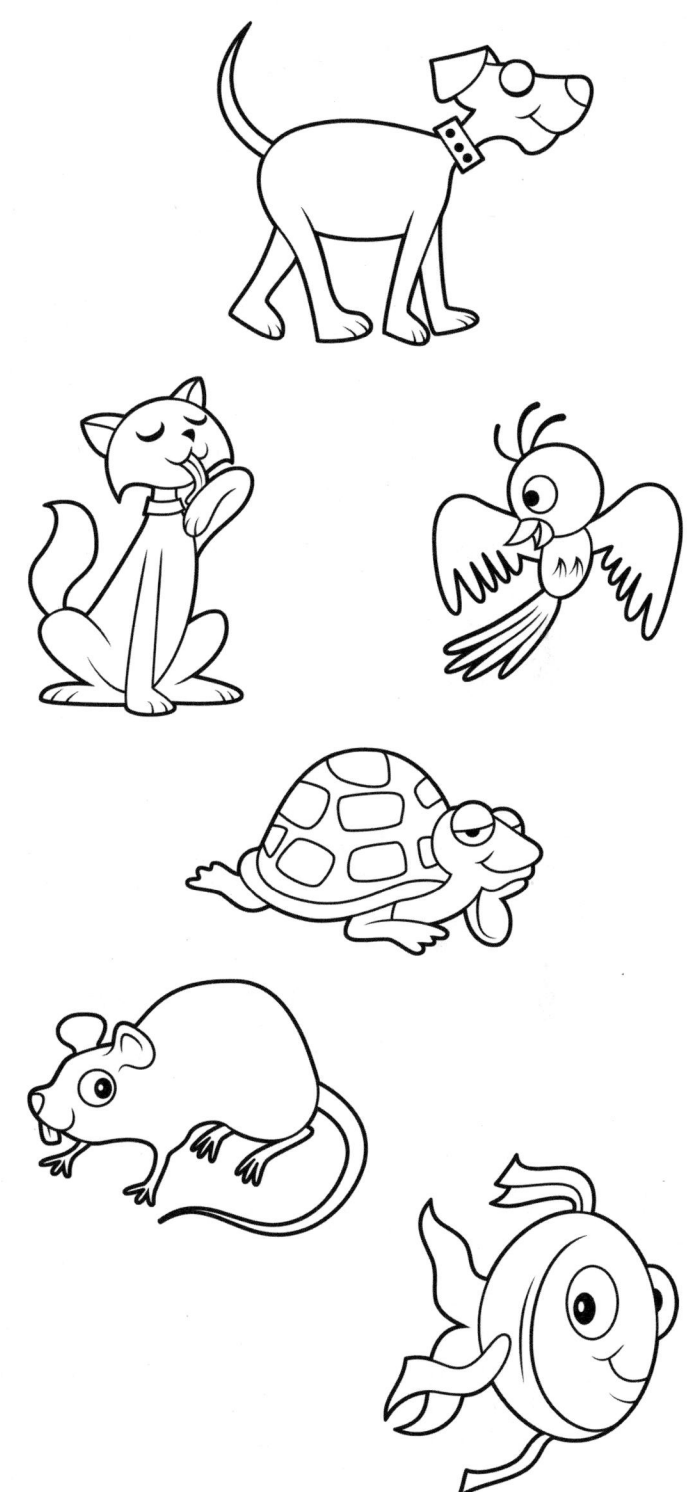

Review: *The dog is (brown).*

9 My Garden

1 Match, colour, and say.

Practice: *flower, nest, tree*

3) **Colour pink.**

4. **Trace and match. Colour.**

1 2 3 4 5

Practice: 1–5, circle, square, triangle

VALUES

5 Trace, colour, and say.

Practice: Play safely.

UNIT 2 PHONICS — Initial *p* sound

Colour and say.

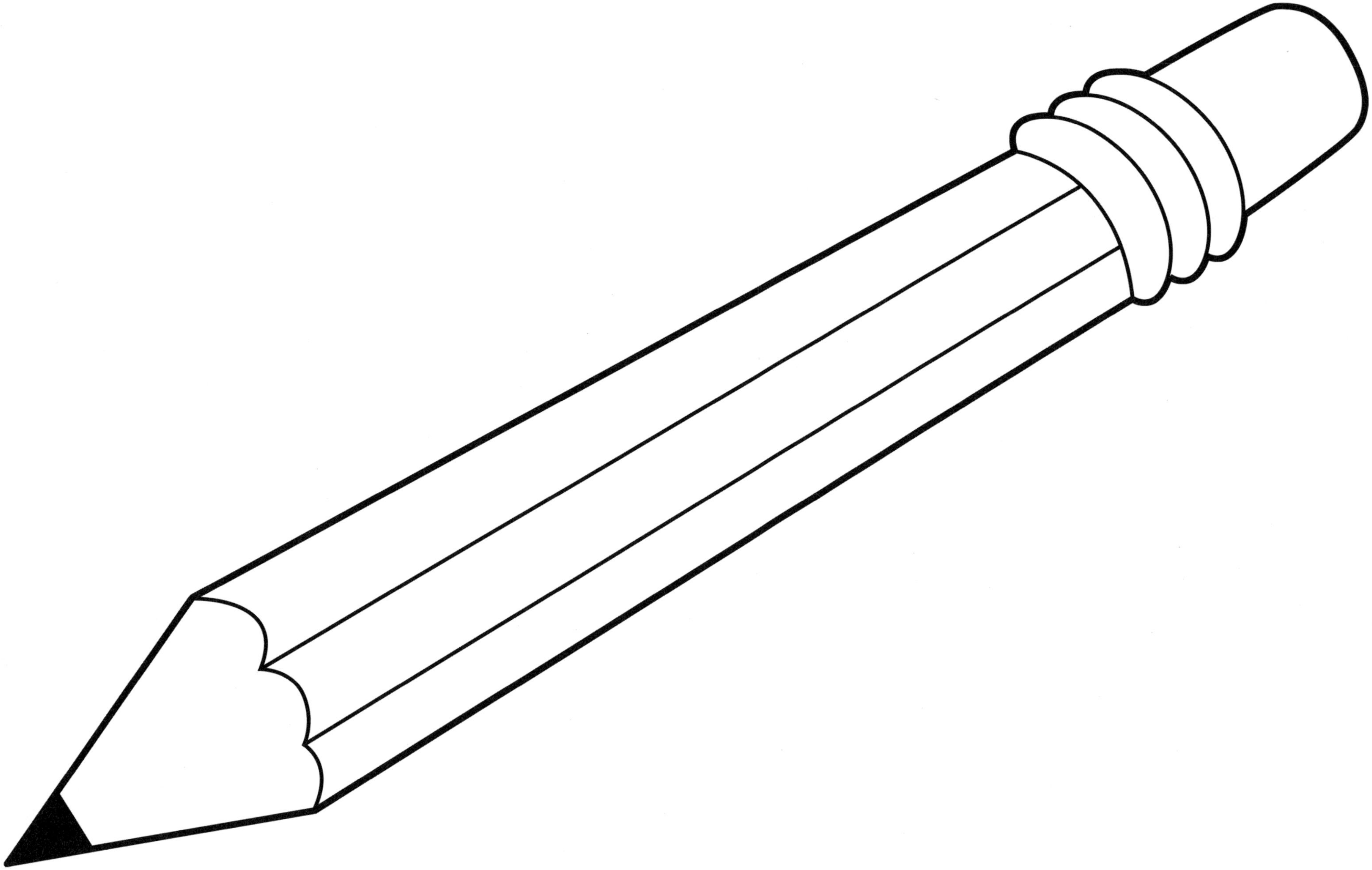

Practice: initial *p* sound in *pencil*

  **Initial *m* sound**

Colour and say.

Practice: initial *m* sound in *me*

UNIT 4 PHONICS — Initial *t* sound

Colour and say.

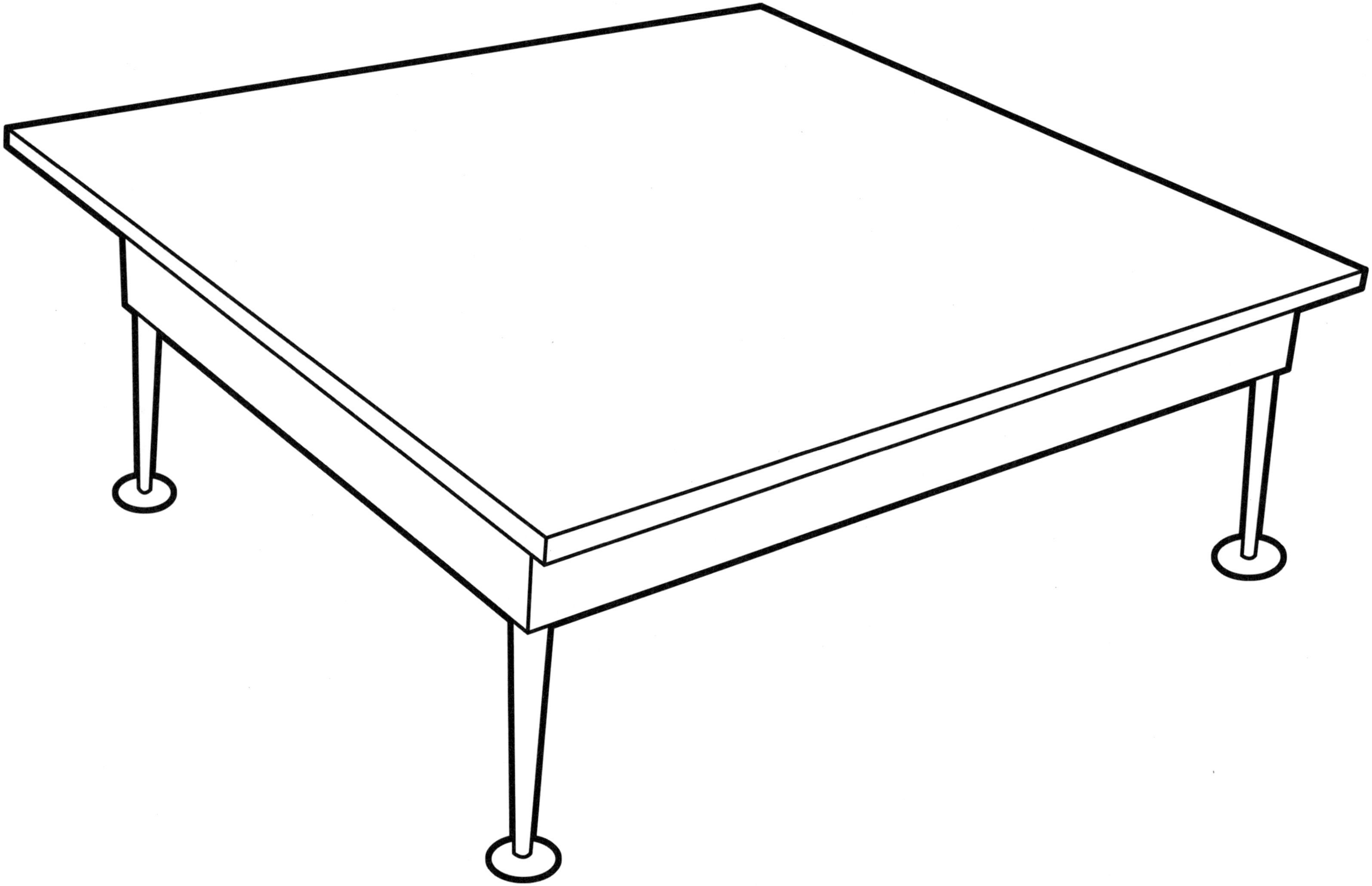

Practice: initial *t* sound in *table*

UNIT 5 PHONICS — Initial *k* sound

Colour and say.

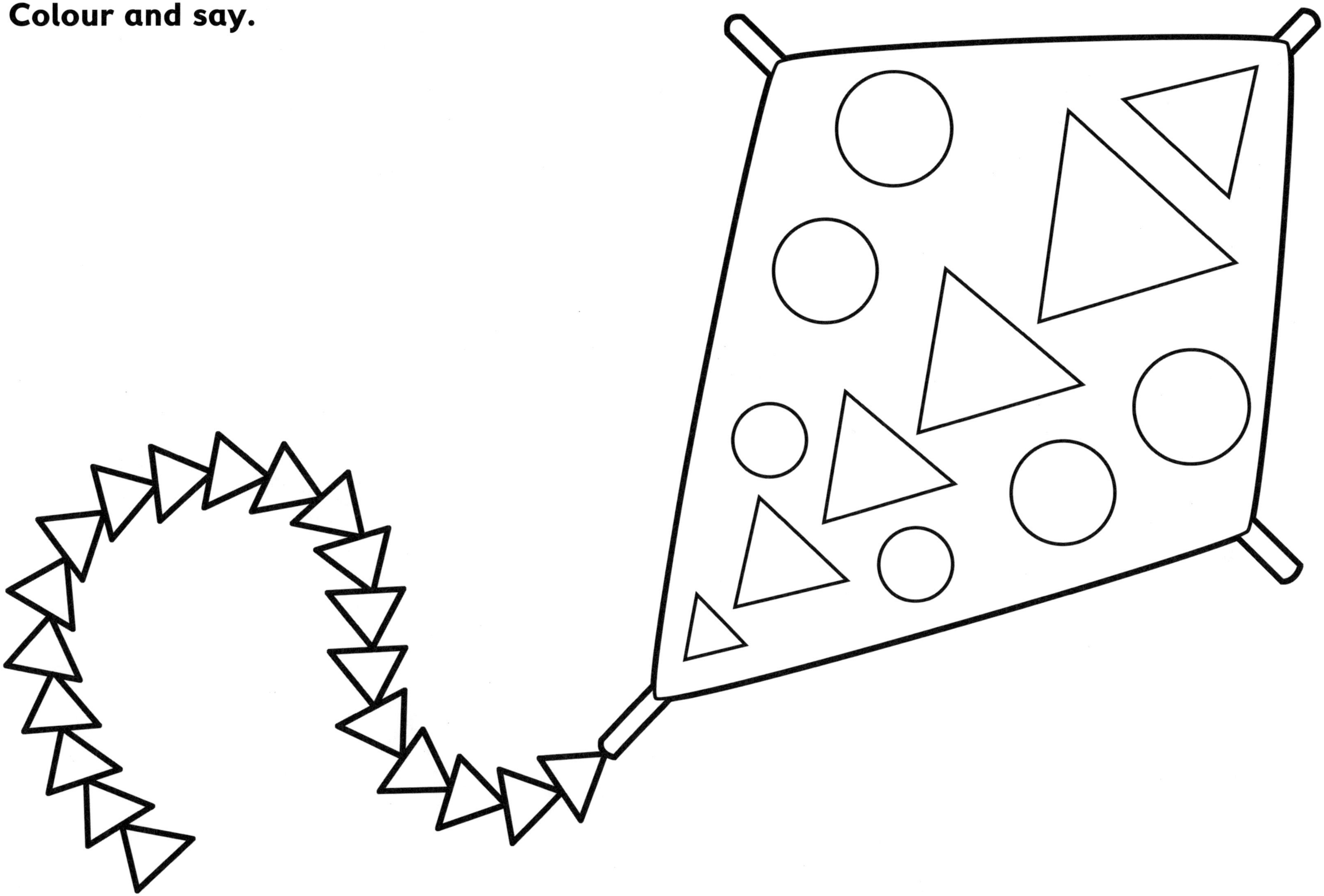

Practice: initial *k* sound in *kite*

UNIT 6 PHONICS — Initial *d* sound

Colour and say.

Practice: initial *d* sound in *dog*

UNIT 7 PHONICS — Initial *l* sound

Colour and say.

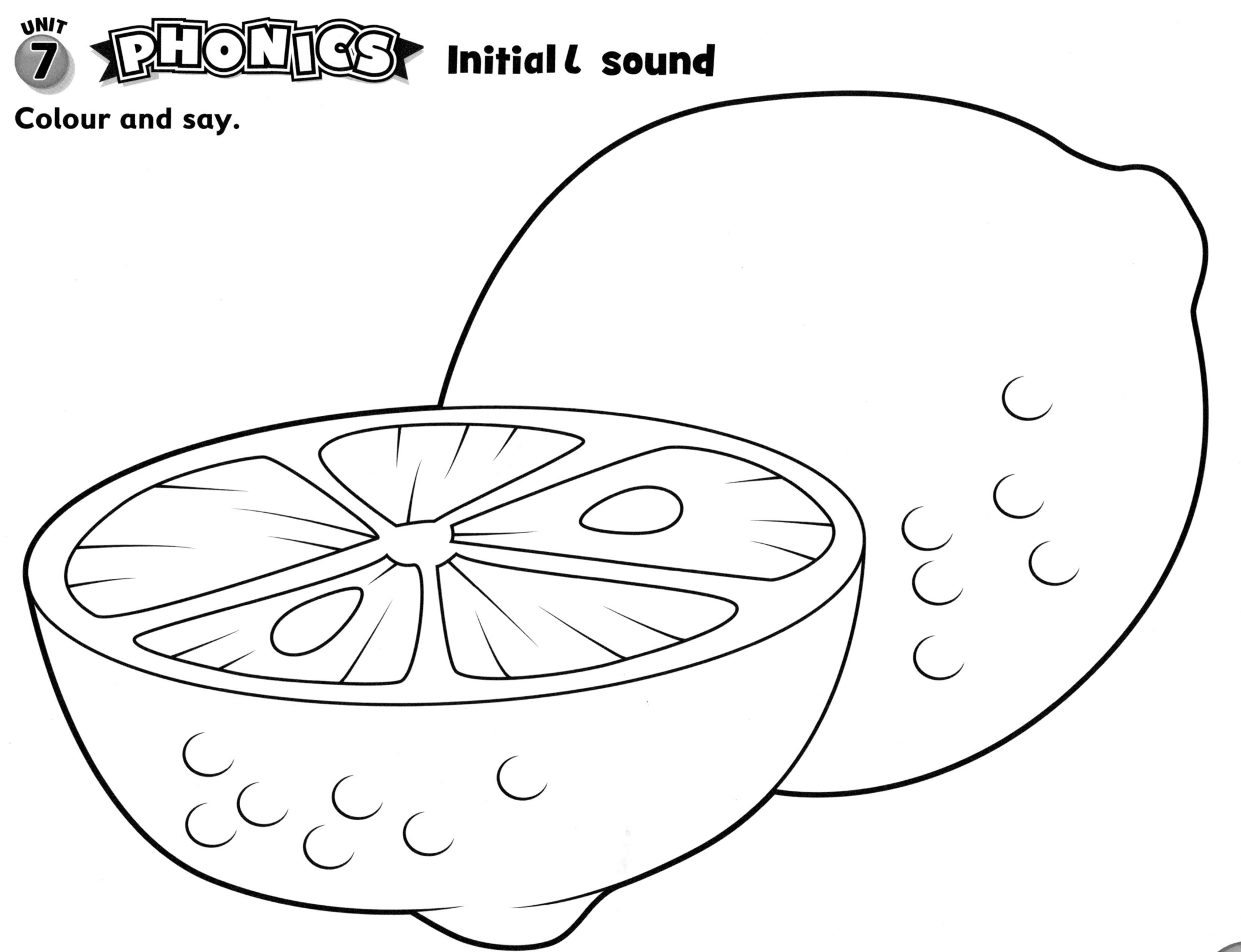

Practice: initial *l* sound in *lemon*

63

UNIT 8 UNIT 9 PHONICS — Initial *b* and *s* sounds

Colour and say.

Practice: initial *b* sound in *bird*, initial *s* sound in *sun*